Go to the
Dragon
maker

Shirley Isherwood

Illustrated by John Prater

OXFORD
UNIVERSITY PRESS

1

The dare

Shaun, his younger brother Michael, and their friend Joe had been playing together since morning. Shaun was the eldest; he was tall and had red hair. Michael was known for his quickness and his chatter. Joe was somewhere in between in age, and was darker and quieter; 'still waters run deep' was what was said about Joe, meaning that there was more to him than met the eye.

Now they were bored, the daylight was fading, and they were just about to go home for tea when they saw the old man. He was tall and thin and he wore a long black coat and a hat with a deep brim; but really they heard him before they saw him – heard the *squeak, squeak, squeak,* of his boots as he made his way down the street. At the sound they turned and saw the figure striding towards them.

When he reached the three boys the old man stopped, and looked at each one in turn.

'Dull,' he said, prodding Joe in the chest with his long finger, on the end of which was a long curved finger-nail, which was more like a claw than a nail.

'Dull,' he said, poking his finger at Michael.

'In the doldrums,' he said, stabbing his finger-nail at Shaun. Shaun stepped back a little way.

'Frightened of me, aren't you?' said the old man, grinning and showing his teeth, which

were yellow and long like his finger-nails.

'No!' said Shaun. 'I just don't like people prodding their fingers at me.'

'And I don't know what doldrums are,' he added.

'I'll tell you,' said the man, putting his face close to Shaun's. 'The doldrums are what you find yourself in when you're at sea, and there is no wind to fill your sails. And so you sit, day after day – nothing happens, nothing can happen . . .'

He stood upright, and it was then that they knew he was a Wizard with the greatest power – for sea birds began to circle overhead, crying, and all three boys could smell the sea. Then the gulls and the sea-smell vanished, and the old man stood there in the darkening street, laughing.

'What you want is something to spark you off – a challenge, a dare, that would be like a strong wind in the sails of a ship to send you off on a great adventure.'

He put his face close to Shaun's once more. This time, Shaun did not step back. He stared into the old man's eyes. 'All right,' he said. 'What's the dare?'

The old man pursed his lips and gazed up, as though he were deep in thought. Joe and

Michael moved closer to Shaun so that they were three together, united.

'Whatever it is, I'm going to do it!' Shaun thought.

'Whatever it is, I'm going to do it!' Michael said to himself.

'Me too!' thought Joe, guessing what the others were thinking.

At last, the old man spoke. Smiling, he reached into a pocket of his coat, and drew out a card, which he handed to Shaun.

'I dare you,' he said. 'I dare you, all three, to go to the Dragon-maker.'

2

Three united

'There's no such person,' said Shaun.

'Look at the card,' said the man. Shaun looked. 'The Dragon-maker,' it read. 'Nab End House.'

Nab End House was a big house which stood on the far side of the canal, next to the Park. It had been built on a rise of land, and could be seen from the street where the boys lived; but the house was empty and had been for many years; its garden was overgrown with weeds and its big iron gates hung half-off their hinges.

Joe and Michael bent their heads to read the card. When all three heads were raised once more the man was walking away up the street.

'I think this is a joke,' said Shaun, looking at the card in his hand.

'I think so too,' said Michael.

'It's not! It's not!' said Joe. He wanted it to be true, and to have an adventure like the man said; a strange, wild, wonderful adventure.

'We've got to go!' he said.

'All right,' said Shaun. 'We'll go. We'll go right now.' He leant over the low wall of the garden for his plastic sword, which lay under a bush. The sword was part of a game which they had invented long ago last summer, and which they now no longer played. But suddenly, he felt as though he must take it with him.

The sword was covered with dirt and spider webs, and he wiped it clean with his hand. Michael and Joe watched him. Neither one spoke, or thought it babyish to want an old, child's toy.

3

Three divided

They trotted down the street in silence, then climbed the steep path which led to the canal. Nab End House looked large and dark on the other side of the water. All around lay the overgrown garden, thick with weeds and thistles, which bordered the Park. The three boys made their way over the canal bridge, and stood in a row for a moment in front of the iron gates. Then they clambered over and walked up the gravel path.

The night seemed not so dark now that they had climbed the rise of land, and looking back they could see below them the silvery stretch of water, and beyond that the village, with the street lights, and the lights of the houses coming on.

'But it's somehow different,' said Michael; but he couldn't explain what the change had been.

Shaun felt it too. 'I think it's a sort of magic,' he said. 'I think some kind of magic's happened.'

As he spoke, a great black bird, a raven, came swooping up from the dusk and settled on the branch of a tree with a loud flap of its wings.

'Three united will be divided,' it croaked in a loud hoarse voice.

'What?' said Shaun. He looked up into the tree and saw the bird's round bright eye

gazing down at him. At that moment, the door of Nab End House was flung open and a large strong net was flung out by an unseen hand. It fell over Joe and he was caught in the mesh and snatched into the house. The door was slammed shut.

Shaun raced up the steps and hammered on the door, but no one answered. Michael fled, running over the wilderness of the garden.

'Mike! Come back!' Shaun cried, but Michael ran on, and disappeared into a mist that drifted up from the canal. 'Oh, Mike . . . !' thought Shaun. He understood his brother very well; Michael could be incredibly brave, but not at times like this when things happened suddenly; he needed time to think.

'He'll be back,' said Shaun. Then he looked up at the raven. 'What shall I do?' he asked.

'Go to the house of the Witch in the Park,' the bird croaked; then he seemed to fall asleep, for the bright eye vanished, quickly, like a little light going out.

Shaun made his way back down the drive and over the rise of land. The canal and village could now no longer be seen. He guessed he must be very near the Park, but he was in a place he had never been before, and he had no idea where the Witch's house might be.

'But I have to find it!' he said, and kept on walking, stumbling over stones and fallen branches in the darkness of the night. Then suddenly the moon came out, and he saw the raven flying towards him. 'How enormous are its wings!' he thought. Feeling a little afraid, he held out his wrist and the bird came down on it.

'I can't find the house,' said Shaun. The raven cocked its head and looked at him with its bright eye. 'It's over there,' it said, and turning to look, Shaun saw a crooked chimney with a wisp of white smoke, and a lighted window in the depths of the trees.

'It wasn't there before!' he said, but the bird continued to cock its head, and looked at him with what appeared to be amusement.

With the raven gripping tight to his wrist, Shaun made his way up the Witch's garden path.

4

Michael and the dragon

When Michael ran he told himself it was
because he didn't want to be caught in the
net. 'If both Joe and I were caught, Shaun
would be left all alone,' he told himself. 'How
could Shaun manage, all on his own? I'll just
run a little way, and then go back and help
him get Joe out!'

But he ran for more than a little way. He
ran as fast as he could, for his legs seemed to
have a mind of their own and wouldn't stop.
Then he ran into a mist which came from
nowhere, and was forced to stop. 'I'm a
coward,' he thought miserably, 'only cowards
run away.'

The mist had gathered more thickly.
Michael supposed that it came from the
canal; but as it swirled around him, he
realized that this was no ordinary fog.

As he stood and wondered, a black, wet

nose came poking through the mist; it had huge nostrils, whence the smelly mist came. As Michael stared, a huge mouth opened beneath the nose, a mouth with long, sharp yellow teeth.

The moon came out, the smelly mist cleared and Michael saw the creature clearly. It was a dragon, and it was enormous, covered in dark green and gold scales.

'Will it eat me?' wondered Michael. 'Will it breathe fire on me?' He was no longer afraid, for there had been time for him to think.

'I shall do neither of those horrible things!' said the dragon, with a great, gusty sigh.

'You read my thoughts!' said Michael.

'All dragons can read thoughts,' said the dragon. 'But that's about the only dragon-thing that I can do.' He sighed again and flopped down onto the ground. He was, thought Michael, for all the world like a great dog who has been told that there was to be no walk that day.

'I'm one of the failed ones,' he said. 'Dragons who can't be fierce.'

'The failed ones?' asked Michael.

'All dragons are made by the Dragon-maker,' the dragon told him, 'and usually they are just what you would expect – fierce, fearless, desperate fighters. Only once a batch of us turned out not as the Dragon-maker wished.'

'What happened?' said Michael. He sat down by the dragon's side and thought of how wonderful it was, suddenly to find himself sitting by a great creature who was supposed to exist only in fairy tales and legends.

'The Dragon-maker was terribly angry,' the dragon went on with a sob, 'and so that we couldn't fly away and disgrace him, he made our wings rather weak. We can fly up into trees but no further. We were hunted,' he said, gazing earnestly into Michael's face. 'Knights came, riding horses.'

'Knights!' exclaimed Michael, very surprised.

'Dragons live for a very long time,' said the dragon.

'I'm glad you weren't captured and killed,' said Michael.

'The Witch in the Park took pity on us. She made us invisible to humans, except those who believe in magic; and hardly anyone does any more,' said the dragon. 'When the Dragon-maker found out he made us invisible to one another also – and deaf to each other as well. And I'm so lonely, and I expect all the other dragons are too.'

A great tear squeezed itself from under his eyelid and rolled down his green and gold face, where it evaporated in a little hiss of steam as it rolled over the black nose. At this, Michael wondered if the dragon could breathe fire, for his nose must be very hot to vaporize great tears.

'Oh, yes,' said the dragon, reading Michael's thoughts once more, and a great plume of flame shot out of his right nostril and burned down a row of thistles. 'But what is being able to breathe fire if one can't see one's friends?' And tear after tear fell and hissed on the hot black nose.

'Please don't cry,' said Michael.

'The Witch told me,' said the dragon, stifling his sobs for a moment, 'that if a boy would catch my tears in a crystal jar with a silver top, then I and my friends could go in search of the Wizard. He would know how to make us visible and brave and strong and – oh, everything that a dragon ought to be.' He looked at Michael, pleadingly.

'But I don't have a crystal jar with a silver top,' said Michael.

'I have one here,' said the dragon quickly, and he held out in his claw a tall jar with a silver top.

'And now,' he went on, lowering his great head, 'I will think of my invisible friends, and weep.'

The tears fell, huge and wet. Michael unscrewed the silver lid, and kneeling, held the jar against the dragon's cheek. The drops fell with a loud *plop!* and in no time at all it seemed, the jar was half full.

Michael held it tightly with both hands, and wondered what the other dragons looked like. Would they be as big as the weeping dragon by his side? Would they all breathe fire? He hoped that Shaun would see them, with Michael in their midst. Then he could not be thought of as a coward, ever!

Something wet and heavy splashed onto his hand. 'The jar is full,' said the dragon. 'Screw on the top, if you please.'

Michael sat down, the crystal jar between his knees. The dragon now seemed quite cheerful.

'There is a time for unhappiness and a time for gladness,' said the dragon, reading Michael's thoughts once more.

Michael smiled at him. It was quite a good trick for the dragon to be able to read his thoughts, for some things were difficult to explain. The right words could be hard to find, and when one tried, people became impatient and said, 'Yes. Yes, I know just what you mean,' even though they did not know in the least what was meant.

'It *is* a good trick, isn't it?' said the dragon, and he puffed out a great sigh of happiness, which smelled of worms and meat and crunched-up bones.

5

Shaun, the Witch and Spellbinder

When Shaun reached the house of the Witch in the Park, the raven tapped on the lighted window with his beak. At once, the door opened by itself with a creaking sound. A voice called, 'Come in. What do you want? State your wishes clearly.'

'Do as she says,' said the raven and with that he rose into the air and flew away into the night. Shaun was sorry to see him go, for he thought that the raven was a bird of great wisdom.

Slowly, Shaun stepped into the room.

A black cat was curled on the rug before the fire, but got up and stretched itself as Shaun entered the room. The Witch herself sat at a table, stirring the contents of a teapot. A great crystal ball stood in the centre. A little pile of cards lay nearby on which were printed these words: *Let me look into your past and your future with the aid of my magic crystal ball.*

'Who sent you?' she asked.

'A big black bird told me to come to you,' said Shaun.

'Ah, my raven,' said the Witch. 'Why did he tell you to come to me?' she added, still stirring the teapot.

Shaun told her about the dare, and how Joe had been caught in a net, and how Michael had run away. The black cat jumped up on to the table and listened to the story with interest.

'So he's back, Spellbinder,' said the Witch to the cat when Shaun had finished. 'The Dragon-maker's back.' She whizzed her spoon round in the teapot more vigorously than ever.

'You're still stirring the tea,' murmured Spellbinder. 'It will be very strong.'

'I like it strong,' snapped the Witch, putting the lid on the pot.

'No, you don't,' replied Spellbinder. 'You hate it.'

Shaun listened to this exchange in astonishment. How could they talk about how strong the tea was going to be when there was a dreadful maker of dragons camped in the old house, and his friend Joe had been caught in a net?

The Witch looked up and caught his eye. She seemed to know what he was thinking.

'It's no use getting agitated and hot-headed,' she said. 'The thing to do is to stay calm, and then act.'

'How?' asked Shaun.

'Well?' said the Witch. 'What do you want? What do you think would help you best?'

Both cat and Witch gazed at Shaun with a calm and steady gaze.

Shaun felt bewildered; there were so many things he could ask for, but which amongst them was the thing which would help him free Joe from the net and find Michael?

'You may sit for a moment while you think,' said the Witch.

Shaun sat down. As he did so, the scabbard of his sword struck against the chair leg. Shaun stood up again.

'I wish that my sword was a real one!' he said.

The Witch stared at him for a moment. 'Hold it up then,' she said. Shaun raised his sword.

'Higher,' she said. 'Above your head.'

Shaun held the sword as high as he could. It seemed to grow very heavy.

'Is the spell working?' he asked.

'The spell? The spell?' said the Witch, getting up from the table and rummaging in a drawer. 'I haven't even found it yet. Where has it got to, Spellbinder?'

'It's in the bottom drawer,' said Spellbinder.

'So it is,' said the Witch. She took something from the drawer, whirled round to face Shaun, and seemed to throw something at him, which glittered and then vanished. Shaun closed his eyes. When he opened them again, the Witch was sitting at her table, pouring a cup of very strong tea.

'So?' she asked, 'what are you waiting for?'

'Is it done?' asked Shaun. 'Is it a real sword now?'

'That's for me to know and you to find out,' said the Witch.

'Perhaps I should go with him,' said Spellbinder. 'Just for a little way.'

'Very well,' said the Witch. 'But only for a little way.'

She put down her cup and snapped her fingers. 'Be gone!' she cried, and at once, Shaun and Spellbinder found themselves in the dark, night Park.

The swiftness of the spell took Shaun's breath away, but Spellbinder seemed quite unaffected. 'She's in one of her brisk moods,' he said, by way of explanation.

Shaun looked at the sword. It still looked like a plastic toy. 'Will it really work?' he asked the cat.

'Her spells nearly always do,' said Spellbinder; he seemed quite unconcerned as to whether the sword was real or not. Shaun took a deep breath, and set off down the path. He did not know if Spellbinder was following him, but he hoped that he was.

6

Joe, Nasty and the Dragon-maker

At first when Joe was captured in the net, he struggled as hard as he could to free himself. But the mesh was strong, so he lay still and curled himself into a ball. As he lay like this he was dragged along a winding, dark, and very cold corridor. After a while he lifted his

head, and twisted it round to see a large gnarled hand that held the mouth of the net closed. He saw too, the flapping tails of a long, black, dusty coat, and the heels of two black boots.

At last they came to a halt by a pair of huge oak doors. 'Open up, Nasty!' cried the man who held the net. 'I've got a choice one here!'

At once, the doors were flung open, and a small squat figure in a blue jerkin stood before him. It was the dwarf, Nasty.

'It doesn't look very choice to me,' he said, crouching and poking a sharp finger at Joe through the meshes of the net. 'Not enough meat on it.'

'We don't intend to eat it,' said the man. 'You know what we want it for – we want it for its boldness. We need its boldness for our dragons.'

'It's over-young,' said Nasty. 'How old is it – let's see. Let's look at its teeth,' and quick as lightning, the sharp finger was thrust into

Joe's mouth, and a squinty, red-rimmed eye was pushed close to his face.

Joe bit the finger – hard. When the finger was removed, he spat in the eye.

'Oh, it's got a temper!' cried Nasty, dancing about and shaking his finger.

The man grinned and bending, took hold of the net, turned it upside down and shook Joe out. He landed on his feet. 'Just like a little cat,' said the man, admiringly.

But Nasty snarled and would have rushed at Joe, had the man not shot out an arm and held him back. He lifted the dwarf up by the scruff of the neck, so that his little black boots dangled just above the ground. Nasty cringed down into his jerkin, sinking lower and lower, until hardly anything of him could be seen save his squinty eyes, and his little red cap with a bobble on the pointed crown.

'You'll not harm him, Nasty,' said the man. 'We need him.' His voice sank lower as he spoke, and suddenly Joe knew who he was.

'You're him!' he said. 'You're the man who told us to go to the Dragon-maker. You *are* the Dragon-maker.'

7

The jar of tears

As Michael and the dragon sat, the moon came out from behind a cloud and shone on the jar of tears. 'How beautiful it looks,' Michael said to himself. 'But what are we to do with it?'

'Take it to the Wizard,' said the dragon. 'He'll know what to do. He lives in the Park, near the Red Rocks. He has his home in a cave there.'

Michael knew the Park well, but even in the day time, he was forbidden to go near the Red Rocks. It was a strange part of the Park, where the rocks rose suddenly, like great cliffs, from amongst the trees.

'Why would anyone live in a cave?' he asked, thinking of how cold and damp and lonely it must be to have your home in such a place.

'The Wizard's spells were stolen by dwarfs

at the Dragon-maker's command. Only they know the passages in the cave, and that's where they hid the spells. Now the Wizard just wanders about, looking for them. Some say that if you stand at the mouth of the cave you can sometimes hear his footsteps and hear his sighs – but he is never seen.'

Michael wondered how the Wizard managed to find things to eat and drink in a cave.

'I think perhaps he's remembered a few simple spells,' said the dragon, 'such as how to conjure up a bowl of porridge.'

The more Michael learned about this Wizard, the more he longed to see the cave, and perhaps hear the footsteps.

'But if the Wizard is never seen,' he said, 'how can we ask him about the jar of tears?'

'We could stand outside and call,' said the dragon, gazing hopefully at Michael.

'All right,' said Michael. He got to his feet, and holding the jar of tears, he set off down the steep path through the Park which led to the Red Rocks. The dragon padded softly by his side.

The Red Rocks looked more forbidding and bigger than ever in the darkness of the night.

'However can we climb up there?' cried Michael.

'I can fly,' the dragon reminded him gently. He knelt, rather in the manner in which a camel kneels so that its rider can mount, and Michael scrambled on to his back.

'Hold tight,' said the dragon, and up they went.

8

The children in the net

Inside Nab End House, the Dragon-maker took hold of the neck of Joe's T-shirt, and led him into the hall beyond the double doors. The dwarf Nasty walked behind, muttering to himself.

As they entered the room, two small figures came hurtling toward them over the flag-stone floor. They were the two dwarfs, Little Crime and Bad Thought. They thrust their twisted faces, as wrinkled and as brown as nuts, close to Joe's.

'Who is it?' asked Little Crime.

'*What* is it?' asked Bad Thought, with a screeching laugh.

'It's a nice little bundle of boldness,' said the Dragon-maker. 'It's got enough boldness in it to make up what we need.'

He turned to the dwarfs. 'It was a bad catch tonight,' he said. 'Timid things you brought me tonight, snivelling, weeping things – hardly any boldness there in the whole net-full.'

'It wonders what you are talking about,' said Bad Thought.

'Shall we tell it?' said Little Crime.

'Do so,' said the Dragon-maker.

'He wants it for the new dragon,' said Bad Thought to Joe, 'and the boldness of small boys is the best.'

'And what does it look like, this boldness?' said Little Crime. 'It sometimes looks like flames, and sometimes like glowing jewels and sometimes like lightning.'

'And how does he get it?' said Nasty. 'How does he extract it? – Ah . . . that would be telling.'

Again he thrust his face close to Joe's. This time Joe kicked him hard in the shin.

'See what I mean?' said the Dragon-maker, as Nasty yelped and hopped about. Bad Thought and Little Crime nodded, and seizing Joe by the arms, they hurried him across the room and bundled him into a net. The net was then raised by a creaking pulley, and Joe found himself swinging gently to and fro from a beam.

A much bigger net swung from the same beam, as packed with small boys as a fishing boat's net is packed with fish. Many pairs of eyes gleamed at him from the meshes, and several small hands reached out and stretched towards him.

'Oh, save us . . . save us!' cried a dozen or more voices.

The net which held them swung wider and wider as the children reached out to Joe. But even though he stretched out his own hands, the net never came near enough for the hands to touch. Below them, in the dusky fire-lit cavern of the hall, the dwarfs watched and danced with glee.

'Swing little fishes, swing in your nets!' they shouted. But after a while the children and Joe realized that they could never reach one another, and slowly the nets ceased to swing.

9

A dragon before morning

As Joe lay quietly in his net he felt something as big as a large pebble, pressing into his back. Squirming round, he found a knot in the mesh. It was tied very tightly, but Joe began to work on it at once. From time to time he glanced below to make sure that the dwarfs hadn't noticed what he was doing. But he was far too high up for them to see, and anyway they were too busy eating and drinking and quarrelling amongst themselves to notice that a boy with nimble fingers was trying to make his escape.

Some hours later, the knot was undone. The hole in the mesh was big enough for Joe to scramble through and clamber up to the beam that held the net.

Below him, the dwarfs were now tired and they huddled together, twitching as they dropped off to sleep. But the children were still awake, and at first they cried out on seeing Joe escape. Then instinct told them to be quiet and they clung to their net and just watched him, their eyes wide with excitement, as he made his way along the beam to the wall.

The wall was made of thick, rough stones. The cement which held them together had crumbled away a little, leaving footholds and fingerholds.

Slowly, holding his breath, Joe made his way down to the bottom. Then he stood, shivering a little from his efforts, and gazed up at the children. They lay, still silent, waiting for him to free them. But then a dreadful thought occurred to him: the net would be very heavy. If he unwound the rope from its peg to let it down, he would not be strong enough to stop it crashing to the floor. He needed someone to help him – a man . . .

'. . . or a dragon,' said a croaky voice from the window-sill.

Looking up, Joe saw the raven that had spoken to Shaun. 'A dragon before morning,' said the bird. 'I will bring you one.' And with that, he spread his great black wings and flew off into the night.

10

Joe's climb

Joe sat crossed-legged in the great hall of the Dragon-maker's house and watched the sky for signs of the dawn. The dwarfs still snored in a corner of the hall, and above him, the children still waited to be rescued. Joe heard the murmur of their voices from time to time.

At last he heard a flapping of wings, and the raven and a dragon settled on the window-sill. At the sight of the dragon the children drew in their breath all together, as though they were one child.

'But he's a rather small dragon,' thought Joe, a little disappointed.

The dragon read his thought at once. 'All dragons are strong, no matter what their size,' came the reply, as the dragon flew down to his side. 'And I'm a she.'

Unwinding the rope from the hook, the dragon began to let down the net. Slowly, slowly it descended; and as it came down, the pulley began to squeak.

It was a very loud squeak and at the sound, one of the dwarfs stirred in his sleep. The dragon looked at Joe.

Joe thought, 'If she pulls the net back up, the pulley will still squeak. But we can't stay with the net neither up nor down.'

There was only one thing to be done; he must find some oil and then climb back up and silence the pulley.

'How brave you are!' whispered the dragon, again reading Joe's thoughts. But Joe was too busy looking on the great littered table for a can of oil to be surprised that a dragon had not only read his mind, but had spoken to him twice.

With the oil can tucked into his jeans pocket, he stood before the wall. It was very high, and grew darker and darker as it rose. Placing his foot in the first gap between the stones, he began his climb. 'Don't look down, don't look down!' he told himself at every step.

Up he went, passing the children in their net, who lay as quiet as mice. He wasn't far from the top when a cold shock went through him – he had reached up his hand, but there was no gap between the stones in which his fingers might lodge. The stones were held firmly together by cement, right to their edges.

'I must have come up a different way from the way I went down,' Joe thought. In the net, the children gasped and one or two began to whimper.

As Joe clung to the wall, a

dragon-thought came up to him. 'Be brave!'
it said. 'Be strong! Hold on!' In the next
moment the raven had flown to his shoulder
and was pecking at the mortar which held
the stones. It fell down, sometimes like
powder, and sometimes in little clumps,
making a frighteningly loud noise as it struck
the floor of the hall.

'Are the dwarfs waking up?' Joe wondered,
and back came the comforting dragon-
thought, 'Fast asleep, every one!'

When the raven had pecked away enough
space for Joe's fingers, Joe began to finish the
climb. His arms and legs were tired, and his
fingers sore from clutching the rough stones,
but at last he reached the beam, crawled
along it and oiled the pulley. Then he
climbed down to the children's net and
clinging to the mesh, he and the children
were lowered carefully to the ground by the
dragon.

'I must go now,' said the dragon. 'Or the
Dragon-maker will find me.'

Then she and the raven flew back to the window-sill and paused there for a moment. 'Good luck! Good luck!' they called softly, before flying away.

'Come on,' said Joe to the children. 'Follow me.'

Opening the great double doors, he began to lead them down the long cold corridor, where he himself had been dragged in his net.

11

The return of boldness

As Joe led the children along the corridor, he could hear the patter of their feet and the soft murmur of their voices. But sometimes the footsteps and the voices stopped and turning, he could see little of the children save their faces, pale as moons some distance away in the darkness of the passage. They clustered together in little frightened groups.

'They have no boldness,' thought Joe. 'The Dragon-maker took it. I must get it back for them.' For he knew that without it, they would never escape from the house. But where could it be?

He remembered the words of Little Crime. *'It sometimes looks like flames, and sometimes like glowing jewels and sometimes like lightning.'*

As he stood and recalled these words, he noticed a large door to his left. There was a gap at the bottom and in the darkness, flashes of light could be seen, sometimes a deep red and sometimes golden. Turning the handle, he entered the room.

The Dragon-maker slept in his armchair. By his side was a small table which held a glass bowl which seemed to be full of fire.

It was not fire, Joe knew, but boldness. As he approached, it foamed and fizzed and spilled over on to the table, but didn't burn either the bundles of papers which lay there, or the edge of the Dragon-maker's sleeve. But the bright crimson light threw deep shadows on the Dragon-maker's face and made him look more fearful than ever.

Holding his breath, Joe took hold of the bowl, and made his way back to the children. As he went, the room behind him fell into inky darkness, and the passageway before him grew lighter. At the sight of Joe and the bowl the faces of the children glowed with happiness.

Not knowing what else to do, Joe threw the fiery contents up into the air and they fell on the children as they clung together. At once, they ran forwards, as happy and as free as children coming out of school at the end of an afternoon. Down the stone corridors and steps they went; then closing the great oak front door behind them, and with Joe at their head, they began to make their way towards the Park.

12

Nasty and company

In the hall of the Dragon-maker, the dwarf, Nasty, awoke and found the empty nets lying on the floor. With a shriek of fury, he ran to find his master. Mucky, Greedy, Little Crime, and Bad Thought woke also and scurried round the empty nets, gibbering like monkeys. They were frightened, for it had been their responsibility to guard the prisoners. What would the Dragon-maker say? What would he do?

The doors of the hall burst open suddenly with a crash and there he stood, holding Nasty by the collar. The dwarfs shrank back in a terrified huddle. Closer and closer to the wall they crept, as slowly, step by menacing step, the Dragon-maker came towards them.

Nasty's boots, just above the floor, made little running movements in the air and he gabbled frantically in a high-pitched voice.

'We'll get 'em, boss. Don't you worry, boss, we'll find 'em. And when we do . . .' The rest of his sentence went unfinished, as the Dragon-maker dropped him to the ground.

'You *will* find them,' said the Dragon-maker. 'You will find them before dawn.' He spoke softly, which was somehow more frightening than if he had shouted and raged. 'And there are the two boys that you must capture as well as the children from the net – Michael and Shaun. I want them all.'

The dwarfs scurried from the hall. The Dragon-maker stood and watched them go.

13

Dragon-flight

While Joe was rescuing the children from the net, Michael and the dragon were making their flight up the Red Rocks. As the dragon had told Michael earlier, he could fly only as high as a tall tree and so they made many stops on little ledges and crags. Each time they came to rest Michael glanced down and saw, with a leap of the heart, how high they had flown. He saw the pale, winding path like a ribbon in the moonlight, and in the distance, the silvery gleam of the canal.

'One more flight, and we will have reached the top,' said the dragon, puffing a little. Michael closed his eyes. He held the jar tightly with his arm flung round it, and with his other hand clutching the ear of the dragon, he felt himself lifted up once more in the cool night air. Then the dragon landed again and came to a halt with three clumsy, running steps.

Michael opened his eyes and found that they stood at the entrance to a cave. Cautiously, they crept a little way inside and called, 'Hello? Anyone there?'

At first they could hear nothing. Then came the far away sound of a pair of shuffling slippers, followed by a gusty sigh.

'He's there!' cried Michael. And he would have run into the cave had not the dragon reached out a claw and held him back.

'A turn or two to the left,' he said. 'A turn or two to the right, and then forget which came first. . .' He left the sentence unfinished.

'You're right,' said Michael. 'I'd never get out.' Then he listened again. 'But the footsteps are going away!' he cried, and indeed, the shuffling sound was so faint that it could scarcely be heard.

At this, the dragon poked his head into the mouth of the cave and sent out a huge tongue of flame. It lit the inside of the cave with a bright red glow, and showed the black openings of many dark passages.

'Again!' cried Michael, when the flame died and the cave had fallen into darkness once more.

The dragon sent out another flame, even bigger, and this time the footsteps could be clearly heard again. A moment later there came the hoarse but happy cry of 'Eureka! I have found them!' and the figure of the Wizard came into sight in the opening of one

of the passages. He was holding a great
bundle of papers tied with string.

'My good, dear dragon,' he said, 'and you,
my good dear sir – by the light of your
wonderful flames I have found my spells.' He
went on, turning to Michael. 'How can I
repay you?'

'What do we do with this jar of tears?'
asked Michael, pointing to the jar which he
had set down in the grass.

'Why, my good fellow,' said the Wizard.
'They are tears, they are sorrow, grief,
unhappiness. Pour them away. Simply pour
them all away.'

Michael knelt and unscrewed the silver lid
and the dragon took the jar in his claw, and
poured the tears onto the ground.

'When will the spell work?' he asked.

'When all the tears have vanished
completely into the earth,' said the Wizard.
All three bent their heads and gazed earnestly
at the little silvery pool. The earth was dry
and hard, and the pool of tears seemed

hardly to diminish at all.

'Patience, patience,' said the Wizard. 'If there is one thing that living in a cave for years has taught me, it is patience.'

14

The name of the sword

Shaun was making his way along the dark paths of the Park. He seemed to have been walking for a long time, but he had no idea of where he should go or what he should do. He thought that Spellbinder was still behind him, but he wasn't sure – from time to time something quick and dark darted across his path, but he couldn't tell if it was a cat or a shadow.

Then suddenly, out of the dark night, he heard whispering and soft, cackling laughter.

It came from a clump of bushes on his left. Shaun drew his sword from its scabbard. It made a metallic sound and Shaun knew then that it had become real. The moon came out and the blade gleamed. The laughter in the bushes stopped.

Spellbinder appeared before him. 'Name it quickly,' he said. 'Your sword must have a

name.'

'A name?' said Shaun, puzzled.

'Yes,' said Spellbinder, 'a name for when
your story is told. "Then Shaun and his

sword went forth. . ." That is how they will tell it, only they will say the name of the sword. Hold it up and say its name.'

It sounded wonderful, thought Shaun, but what name should he choose?

'Quickly!' said Spellbinder. 'That laughter you heard was Nasty and Little Crime, two of the Dragon-maker's most evil dwarfs. Name it quickly or it will change back into a plastic toy.'

'I didn't know that it would change back,' said Shaun. 'The Witch didn't tell me that.'

'She wouldn't,' said Spellbinder. 'She likes to give these little surprises.'

Shaun held the sword above his head. 'You must give it a name that no sword had before,' Spellbinder told him. 'You must give it its rightful name.'

'I name thee Boldness,' said Shaun.

'Been done,' said the cackling voice of Nasty, from the bush. 'Boldness lies rusting in the cave at the Red Rocks.'

'Brave Blade!' said Shaun.

'Same place,' said the cackly voice. 'Hangs from the next nail.'

The whispering began again. The dwarfs were making their plan. Twigs snapped and leaves rustled as they moved about, getting into position to capture him.

'Avenger!' cried Shaun, and at this the laughter grew louder and louder.

Shaun's arm was growing tired with the weight of the sword, but he managed to keep it held high, and it gleamed in the light of the moon. By a shaft of moonlight, he saw Nasty and Little Crime leap from the bush to stand straddle-legged in the path.

'Cold Terror!' cried Shaun, brandishing the sword.

At this, Nasty gave a loud shriek and scrambled into the undergrowth. Little Crime scrambled in behind him.

'He's named it,' snarled Nasty. 'He's found the right name.'

The voices in the bush ceased at this, and all was silent.

'Is it the right name?' Shaun asked Spellbinder.

'Try it and see,' said the cat; he was sitting in the middle of the path, calmly washing his left ear.

The muttering in the bush began again. 'Be silent!' cried Shaun, making a stroke with the sword. The blade flashed through the air, a little nearer to the bush than Shaun had intended; the tips of three branches fell to the ground, together with the grubby bobble that had been stitched to Nasty's hat. Shaun advanced, flourishing Cold Terror, and at the sight of this the dwarfs broke from cover and

ran. Soon, they were lost in the blackness of the night.

'It is the right one,' said Shaun, flourishing the sword again and again with delight.

'So it would seem,' said Spellbinder coolly.

Michael saw the flash of the blade, as he stood at the top of the Red Rocks. Then the clouds uncovered the moon entirely and he saw Shaun holding Cold Terror.

Joe, making his way through the dark Park with the children, saw him too.

The three were once again united.

15

The Dark One

When Nasty and Little Crime reached Nab
End, they hurried at once to the Dragon-
maker. They found him with the net-mender,
Skrimshanks, who was dolefully examining
the hole in the net. He had made the net a
long time ago and had been brought in
earlier to mend the hole. This he had done
by tying the large knot, which Joe had
undone.

'I want it mended properly this time,' said
the Dragon-maker. He spoke quite calmly, but
both Nasty and Little Crime knew that he
was very angry and that as soon as the net
was mended, Skrimshanks himself would be
hoisted up in it. They were glad that
Skrimshanks was in trouble, as this, they
thought, would turn the Dragon-maker's
anger away from themselves; or at least, they

would not have to bear the full force of it.

They were mistaken. The Dragon-maker turned to look at them when they told him what had happened, and his eyes became as cold as ice – ice in which two red flames were darting.

'He found the right name for his sword,' stammered Nasty, shrinking back behind Little Crime.

'You ought to have captured him before he found the name,' snarled the Dragon-maker. He turned to Skrimshanks. 'Be quick with that net!' he said – and both Nasty and Little Crime knew that they would join the net-maker in hanging from the high beam. Little Crime whimpered and Nasty flung himself at the Dragon-maker's feet.

The Dragon-maker nudged him with his toe. 'Get up, groveller,' he snapped. Then he whirled round and strode from the hall, dragging the terrified dwarf behind him. 'There is still time before dawn,' he said as he went. 'And since you have all failed me, I must use my last and my most terrible weapon. I must release the Dark One.'

They reached a great barred door. The bolts were withdrawn, and wrapping his cloak round him, the Dragon-maker strode into the darkness of the room.

*   *   *

Long ago, the Park had been a wilderness of trees and undergrowth. Bears had wandered there, wolves had prowled. In those days, young knights would dare one another to seek out and fight the Dark One. Sometimes they decided by themselves that they would do this to make a great name for themselves.

Many set out, over the years, but none returned and their spirits haunted the Park.

They did not do this to frighten people, but to warn anyone who was foolhardy enough to try to overcome the terrible creature. For many years they drifted along the moonlit paths, gleaming in their ghostly armour, but they never met anyone so rash as to make the attempt, for it had long been accepted that the Dark One was unconquerable.

Some said that the Dark One was not of the Dragon-maker's making, that he had existed long before the Dragon-maker came to live at Nab End House and that the Dragon-maker had simply chanced upon a way to trap him. All anyone knew was that he kept the great dragon in an underground prison, deep beneath the house.

By this time, the knights merely sat in the trees, sometimes alone and sometimes in little groups – which is probably why ghostly knights are never seen, for no one thinks to look for such a thing in a tree.

But on the night that Shaun vanquished Nasty and Little Crime, word was passed from branch to branch that two of the Dragon-maker's dwarfs had been defeated and that the Dragon-maker was sending out the Dark One in revenge.

With a faint, ghostly clanking sound, the knights dropped from the trees and began to make their way to various parts of the Park. A group of three met Shaun as he came along the path that led past the Red Rocks.

'Well met, Fellow!' they cried, snapping open their visors and smiling broadly so that he would not be afraid.

But to meet suddenly with three figures in faintly shimmering armour is alarming, whether they are smiling or not.

Shaun drew Cold Terror and stood, bracing himself for he knew not what.

16
Stand firm!

At that moment, the Dark One came swooping over the Park. Everyone heard the loud beating of his wings, felt the rush of air that bent the treetops. Two bright golden beams of light from the Dark One's eyes lit the path where Shaun stood.

At this, small animals that were abroad on the path, froze in fear.

Joe and the children crouched down in the bushes. All held their breath.

The three knights drew their swords. Although they knew that they could do little with them, save brandish them in a ghostly fashion, they had a faint hope that the Dark One might be fooled by their action. (But they knew in their heart of hearts that he would not.) All they could do to help Shaun was to shout encouragement, and even this came only as a faint echo on the night breeze.

But Shaun heard the words 'Stand firm!' and so he stood his ground, with Cold Terror raised.

The Dark One, swooping down, saw this brave sight. It astonished him so much that he stalled in the air, veered madly to the left and then to the right.

Then the great dragon turned

and began to fly back back to where Shaun stood. This time he snarled as he approached. But again, Shaun stood firm, helped this time by whole families of small night hunters, who had hurried from the grass to hang on to the laces of his trainers.

The little creatures had seen many of their friends and relations snatched up by the cruel talons of hawks, and saw the Dark One as a sort of super hawk, one capable of carrying off a human. They hoped that their weight would make it difficult, if not impossible for Shaun to be carried off. Their bravery and their good intentions helped rather more than their weight.

Spellbinder came from the shadows and stood with his back arched, hissing and spitting.

As the Dark One flew back, Shaun flourished Cold Terror once more, and the Dark One, startled, turned again. He had not expected a boy to stand up to him in this manner, or indeed in any manner.

At the sight of Shaun and Spellbinder standing alone, Joe and the children ran from the bushes.

'We've got to help them!' said Joe. 'But how?'

'We could throw stones!' said the smallest child. But even as he bent and picked up a handful of small pebbles, he knew that they would not be enough and let them fall back to the ground.

17

The battle

At the top of the Red Rocks, Michael, the Wizard and the dragon watched as at last the tears vanished into the ground.

'And now, my dear,' said the Wizard, 'you are everything a good and brave dragon ought to be and you are able to see and hear your friends.'

The dragon raised his great head and gave a loud cry. It was answered by dragon-cries from far away. The dragon gave an answering shout of delight, spread his wings and flew off into the night.

Michael stood at the edge of the rocks and waved until the dark shape of the dragon could no longer be seen. Then, quite suddenly, the moonlit sky darkened, as though a great cloud passed overhead and there was the sound of great wings beating. Looking down, he saw his brother, Shaun, standing before the Dark One, his sword raised in his hand.

He saw too, Spellbinder, spitting, and the small animals clustered round Shaun's trainers. He saw his friend Joe and the children come running from the bushes, armed with nothing more than twigs and branches.

'Can't you do something?' asked Michael in despair, knowing that no one could hold out much longer.

'My dear thing, of course,' said the Wizard, untying his roll of papers and riffling through the dusty pages. 'I've been without my spells for so long that I forget that I now have them . . .'

'Ah!' he went on, stopping and shaking out a sheet. 'Here it is. *To arm anyone, or anything, against evil, no matter how strong . . .*'

He muttered to himself for a moment, then standing perilously close to the edge of the rocks, flung out his hands.

At once Joe and the children were armed

with swords and Spellbinder and the small
animals with the strength of lions. But the
great wings of the Dark One beat them back;

then the dragon turned to face Shaun once more.

'Oh, I wish I was down there with everyone!' cried Michael.

'Nothing easier, old thing,' said the Wizard and in the next instant Michael found himself standing by Joe's side. But he was empty-handed.

'I haven't got a sword!' he shouted, looking up to where he could see the outline of the Wizard standing on the rocks.

'Apologies, old chap,' floated down the voice of the Wizard and a sword appeared in Michael's hand.

'Okay!' said Joe. 'Let's get that Dark One.'

'Let's!' cried Michael.

'Let's!' cried all the children.

But despite three lion-brave voles clinging to his foot, the claws of Spellbinder and the swords that rushed at him from every side, the Dark One seemed as strong as ever.

'What shall we do?' Michael asked Joe, as, with the black wings beating before them, they were driven back, step by step, together with the other children, leaving Shaun standing alone in the path with Spellbinder and the small animals.

18

Dragon fire

In his house, the Dragon-maker, gazing into his crystal ball, heard and saw everything that had happened. As he watched, Bad Thought scurried round him bringing him things which he did not want in the least, his slippers, a plate of toast, a small woollen cap. The Dragon-maker brushed these things aside. 'All I want is time,' he snarled. 'The Dark One cannot exist outside after the dawn breaks.'

This was a flaw in his most terrible weapon and Bad Thought instinctively knew this; but the dwarf was wise enough not to ask more about it.

'Ah, he'll finish off those kids in no time,' he said, restoring the buttered toast to its plate and flicking away bits of fluff and grit.

'But the boy found the right name for his sword,' said the Dragon-maker in an ominously quiet voice. 'Nasty and Little Crime were crouching in the bushes like cowards when he found it.'

'It's just a little bit of magic he got,' said Bad Thought. 'Got it by accident, sheer luck. It won't last.'

'You fool!' said the Dragon-maker. 'Don't you see – it *is* lasting. How else could a mere boy stand up to such danger? It is lasting because he believes in it.'

'Can't we make him stop believing?' asked Bad Thought.

The Dragon-maker smiled. *'We?'* he said. 'You mean *you*.'

Turning to the hook that held the rope, the Dragon-maker began to let down the net that held Nasty, Little Crime and Skrimshanks.

All three were amazed at their release. 'He needs us,' came the cunning thought in Nasty's head and in this he was correct.

'Get the rest of you,' said the Dragon-maker. 'Go to the Park, and find a way to destroy that boy Shaun's belief before dawn.'

'Sure thing, boss,' said Nasty, as he and Bad Thought, Little Crime, Mucky and Greedy hurried away.

The Dragon-maker then turned to Skrimshanks. 'As for you,' he went on, lifting the net from the hook, 'mend this, and mend it properly this time. It will be needed.'

But as the dwarfs made their way down the steep path towards the Park, the sky on the far horizon was lit by a red-gold light.

'That's dragon fire!' muttered the Dragon-maker, gazing into the crystal ball. 'It is dragon fire . . .'

Jumping to his feet and striding across the room, he struggled a moment with the heavy window and then flung it open. 'Dragon fire!' he shouted. 'Do your work, Dark One. Spare none of them! But do it quickly! The dragons are very close!'

His voice echoed over the Park; all heard it. Then the sky grew brighter, as though lit by a hundred flames, and Michael saw his dragon, breathing fire, surrounded by all his long-lost friends and flying

towards them
with great speed. Their beating wings flattened the grass, made the trees wave their branches as if in a gale. Some of the smaller children found it hard to stand upright and the lighter of the little night creatures were blown head over tail along the path.

Shaun stood with his feet braced and with Cold Terror raised and ready to strike. And then the dragons were upon the Dark One. His black body was hidden for a moment by the green and gold of their scales. Like an evil volcano erupting, he burst free and the dragons were flung aside like toys for all their size.

'You're strong now!' cried Michael, dashing dangerously close to where the Dark One stood at bay and to where the dragons breathed out tongues of flame. It was their first fight and they were not yet sure of their strength, prowess and courage.

'You can do it!' cried Michael. 'You can do all that dragons can do!'

When they heard these words the dragons raised their heads and attacked again, their fire blazing. Turning, the Dark One tried to make one last fatal swoop on Shaun, the red-gold glow of dragon fire shining in his eyes. For a moment he hung in the air, like a great black cloud, then the cloud became fine ash

that floated gently to the ground. He was
dead.

'Oh, how brave you all are!' cried Michael,
but even as he spoke, the dragons rose up
and flew in the direction of Nab End House.

19

The end of the magic

As soon as the last of the black ash drifted away, Shaun lowered his sword. His arms were aching and he felt tired. His brother Michael, Joe and the children all crowded round him.

*   *   *

Skrimshanks was making his way along the path which led to his cottage, dragging the heavy net behind him, when he too saw the sky turn red. Nab End House stood on its rise of land to his left, and hearing the sound of the window flung open, he turned his head, and saw the Dragon-maker leaning over the sill, heard his hoarse voice shouting, 'Dragon fire!'

He saw the dragons fly towards the Dragon-maker, their nostrils wide and

breathing flame; and he saw the Dragon-
maker try in vain to close the heavy window.
A moment later something charred and wispy
floated down to the canal, like a scrap of
burnt paper. The Dragon-maker had
disappeared for ever.

'Well,' thought Skrimshanks, 'you made
something there that you couldn't control.'

He looked down at the rope that he held
wrapped round his hand and at the tangled
mass of the net that lay by his feet. He felt
ashamed that he had made it for such an evil
purpose; but then a second thought came to
him. Now the Dragon-maker was gone he
might well find another use for it. He carried
on along the path to his cottage, dragging
the net behind him.

*   *   *

The dwarfs, on their way to the Park, also saw
the dragons breathing fire and they saw the
Dragon-maker fall from the window of the

house.

'What are we going to do, what are we going to do?' cried Bad Thought. Mucky and Greedy clung together, whimpering; Little Crime just walked round in circles. 'Oh boy, oh boy, oh boy,' he said over and over again. Without the Dragon-maker they were lost. Nasty alone remained cool.

'There's a place we can go,' he said. 'I know where it is. Quickly!' They obeyed him at once and without question; someone was in control, that was all they needed or wanted.

Nasty, leading his little huddled band thought, 'Now *I'm* in charge. And I know a thing or two. I kept my eyes and ears open.'

'Turn right here,' he said, reaching the end of the lane.

'Sure thing, boss,' said the dwarfs. 'Sure thing.'

*　　*　　*

Michael sat with his dragon. It was time to say goodbye.

'Couldn't you stay?' Michael asked. 'You could live in the Park, and I could come and visit you. . .'

'But I am a dragon,' said the dragon gently, 'and you are a boy. We can only be together for this short, magical time. My friends are waiting for me.' He waved his claw to where ten green dragons sat, waiting patiently.

'I know,' said Michael, and he flung his arms round the dragon's neck. 'Goodbye!'

The dragons rose then, like a flock of great birds and were soon lost to sight in the night sky.

Michael went to join Joe, Shaun, Spellbinder and the children. The ghostly knights were also there, but were fading until they were nothing more than wisps of mist. 'Goodbye!' came their voices, faintly, followed by three faint, but heart-felt cheers.

'Everyone's saying goodbye,' said Michael. He felt a little tearful and was afraid of crying in front of the others. If he cried, he thought, it would undo all the brave things that he had done.

'Not so . . . not so!' came the voice of his dragon. 'A brave thing done is always there . . .'

'Oh, thank you!' thought Michael, amazed and happy that he and his dragon could still read one another's minds even though they were apart. 'Will we always be able?' he asked.

'Always . . .' came back the answer.

'Here's someone to say "Hello!"' said Spellbinder, and turning their heads, the children saw the Witch hurrying along the path. She was carrying a little china dish, which she tapped with a spoon. The raven sat on her shoulder.

'*There* you are,' she said, seeing Spellbinder. 'Fish for supper, and I've been tapping your dish for the past hour to call you.'

Everyone smiled to think that the tapping of a china dish with a spoon could have been heard amongst the roaring and snarling, the snapping, and the clashing of swords.

The children were still talking about their adventure and their escape from the net, but now they were growing sleepy; and the wonderful swords given to them by the Wizard had vanished. They scarcely seemed to notice. Little by little, the whole thing would seem like a dream.

Soon they would forget.

Everyone began to make their way back to the village. The tea time lights came on in the houses and it was as if the magical night had never been, and they were just a crowd of children going home.

But there was still some magic left in the shape of the old Wizard, the Witch, her cat and her raven.

The Wizard was to be the Witch's guest for a time and they turned off up the little path which led to her house.

Shaun crouched and stroked Spellbinder's head. He felt sad at saying goodbye to the beautiful and bold animal.

'Oh, you'll see him again,' said the Witch, 'but as all black cats look more or less alike, you will never be quite sure that it is him.'

'She does like her little joke,' purred Spellbinder in Shaun's ear. 'But I will let you know. I will give you a sign.'

The raven cawed 'Goodbye!' and flew off into the night. Shaun stood up. 'Come on,' he said to Michael and Joe. 'Let's go.' He glanced down at his sword, which he still held, but which had now turned back into a plastic toy.

'I'll throw it away,' he thought; but as he raised his arm he was struck with an idea and instead, he hung the sword from a branch of a tree.

'Some other child might find it and give it a name,' he said. 'And I hope whoever it is has a wonderful adventure.'

Then together, the three ran all the way home.

About the author

One day last summer, three
small boys paid me a visit:
Joe who lives next door,
and Shaun and Michael,
who live next door but
one. They asked if I 'made
books'. When I replied that
I did, they asked if I would make a book
for them. I said, 'Certainly, what would you like
the book to be about?' and they said 'Dragons!'

I well might have delayed in writing this story
about dragons, being involved with another piece
of work at the time, but all through the summer
Joe, Shaun and Michael presented themselves on
my doorstep, to ask how many words I'd written.
And it was no use plucking a figure from the air,
for they always remembered the previous figure
that they'd been given. So, I wrote *Go to the
Dragon-maker*.